Cryptocurrency in a Nutshell

Cryptocurrency

S. singh Somlok

1956-2013

Contents

....2
Introduction 2
2. 2
....2
Bitcoin, the first cryptocurrency 2
2.1 Bitcoin's creation...2
2.2 The philosophies behind Bitcoin 2
2.3 Working mechanism of Bitcoin..2
2.3.1 Proof-of-Work protocol..2
2.3.2 How does Proof-of-Work and the blockchain allow Bitcoin's network to function? 2
2.4 Bitcoin's promise of security..2
2.5 Fairness in Bitcoin distribution...2
2.6 Detractor's arguments against Bitcoin 2
2.7 Bitcoin as a store of value...2
2.8 Adoption across the world..2
3. 2
....2
Blockchain 2
3.1 Cryptography techniques 2
3.2 Cryptographic hash properties..2

3.3 Immutability 2
3.4 Solving the double-spending dilemma 2
4. 2
.... 2
Types of Cryptocurrencies available 2
4.1 Security tokens 2
4.2 Mining-based coins 2
4.3 Utility Tokens 2
5. 2
.... 2
Blockchain applications 2
5.1 Financial services 2
5.2 Smart contracts 2
5.3 Supply chain applications 2
6. 2
.... 2
Conclusion 2
1. 1

1. Introduction

Cryptocurrencies have become increasingly popular in the late 2010s due to the meteoric rise of cryptocurrencies that saw the price of a single Bitcoin hit $20,000. This generated interest from both retail and institutional investors and it has since become a popular investment asset class. However, not much is known about the cryptocurrency market. Bitcoin has become synonymous with cryptocurrency despite there being thousands of other digital currencies available due to the lack of understanding of what cryptocurrencies are. Much less is known about blockchains, which are the technology that differentiates cryptocurrencies from traditional currencies.

Bitcoin was first introduced to the world in 2009 and has since inspired the creation of many other projects that utilizes blockchain technology as well. It provides both security, immutability, and efficiency which makes it an excellent contender to traditional currencies used today. Contrary to popular belief, cryptocurrencies have a multitude of uses apart from being used for transactions. There are supply chain, data management, contractual transactions, decentralized finance, and remittance applications available today on the market. The advances in blockchain technology will herald a huge shift in our world's economies and the way businesses are conducted can be changed forever.

My name is Greg Somlok and I have been involved in the cryptocurrency industry since 2012. I am currently a successful trader that specializes in cryptocurrency markets and have garnered a wealth of knowledge in both cryptocurrencies and blockchains. It is my belief that a new world is taking shape with the introduction of cryptocurrencies. The industry has seen massive movements around the world to hinder the adoption of digital currencies, such as China's ban of using cryptocurrencies for transactions. Despite the obstacles faced, adoption of this new technology has been on the rise and like it or not, digital currency is here to stay.

2. Bitcoin, the first cryptocurrency

Bitcoin is widely regarded as the father of all cryptocurrencies as it was among the first of its kind and has been the most successful at being recognized as usable currency. Today, it sits at a price of $9,900 (as of 8/5/2020), with a market capitalization of about $180 billion. It has come a long way since its inception back in 2009. Today, it is viewed as a viable investment and has been compared to digital gold. Majority of the world identifies the use case of Bitcoin as an alternative to gold and traditional currencies. However, there is much more to Bitcoin and it will be further discussed in this chapter.

2.1 Bitcoin's creation

Bitcoin was created on the 3rd of January, 2009, seemingly as a reaction to the irresponsible financial policies instituted in the aftermath of the 2008 Financial Crisis. The mortgage loan bubble saw many banks on the verge of being insolvent. This was exacerbated by a run on banks as masses of people rushed to withdraw their money from their banks. Many people lost large portions of their hard-earned savings as markets crashed. Businesses began to mass retrenchments and many lost their livelihoods.

Despite clear evidence of irresponsible fiscal management, banks were bailed out by the government again, which led to many becoming disillusioned with the state of monetary affairs at that point in time. Bitcoin was then created by a founder who had lost faith in world financial systems. The creator who was known as Satoshi Nakamoto then mined the first block in the Bitcoin blockchain. In the genesis block, a text was found that read "The Times 3/Jan/2009 Chancellor on brink of second bailout for banks". At the time of creation, a rule was imposed on the cryptocurrency where only a total of 21 million will be mined into existence. This will play a large part in the value proposition of Bitcoin today.

2.2 The philosophies behind Bitcoin

Bitcoin is created to be decentralized which means that it is not controlled by any single entities. No one will be able to issue new currency and there will be no institution that enacts policies for the new-age currency. Instead, all rules for the cryptocurrency will be determined at the very beginning and the digital currency will stay true to its principles until today.

The founder of Bitcoin created it as a tool of liberation from the corrupt financial systems of today. Current financial systems clearly favor the rich and wealth can be decimated overnight through careless implementation of policies. The market crash in 2008 saw many businesses going bankrupt and the entire stock market lost about half its value. Nakamoto saw us as slaves to the capitalist systems and were at the whims of government regulators who were willing to provide aid to large corporations but were seemingly indifferent to the poor and unemployed. Hence, Bitcoin serves as a currency for those who are seeking an alternate monetary system from traditional currencies which allows them to enjoy a system of fairness for all with no biases.

Thus, Bitcoin is made to be a deflationary currency compared to the dollar, where traditional currencies are printed daily to represent improvements in productivity. Bitcoin however, will become increasingly scarce with each passing day and will thus increase in value with daily productivity increases if adopted as legal tender. This not only helps preserve our assets but also does away with the regressive effect of inflation that hurts the poor.

Bitcoin's unique deflationary characteristic has allowed it to be used to liberate citizens of repressive regimes. Through Bitcoin, people are able to hide their assets from governmental bodies and can preserve the value of their assets. They will be insulated from extremely careless handling of fiscal policies by despots which typically ends in hyperinflation. Bitcoin has been successfully used as a defense against hyperinflation as seen in Venezuela. Venezuelans experienced hyperinflation that started out in 2016 and exceeded 1,000,000% by 2018. Assets were rendered worthless and the economy was in shambles. The country reported monthly wages for workers to be at $2 and the economy simply could not recover because no worker would be willing to work when the value of their salary could disappear by the very next day.

In addition to Venezuela, countries such as the rogue state of North Korea have been reportedly mining and hoarding Bitcoin as a hedge against possible damages against its economy. International organizations who are seeking to provide aid to people in countries of corrupt and incapable governments have also turned to using Bitcoin to purchase supplies for distribution in the country. This allows vendors to retain their earnings and conduct business at fair prices. Current various uses have already shown that Bitcoin can be a viable currency and is an effective driver of financial liberation.

2.3 Working mechanism of Bitcoin

Bitcoin is created through a process called mining. What is not understood by many is how virtual currencies can be mined just like the precious metals on Earth. However, the mining referred to by cryptocurrency enthusiasts do not actually point towards the physical act of mining. Virtual mining is something completely different and relies on computational power instead of physical labor. Followers of cryptocurrency markets are also likely to have heard of the "Proof-of-Work" mechanism used by Bitcoin. Much of this jargon may seem confusing at first, but will make complete sense once the entire working mechanism of Bitcoin is understood.

2.3.1 Proof-of-Work protocol

The Proof-of-Work protocol that allows a majority of cryptocurrencies to function today refers to a consensus mechanism, whereby miners provide the Bitcoin network with their computational power and are compensated with block rewards in return. Large amounts of processing power is used to solve difficult computational puzzles which is used to confirm transactions in the network. Consequently, new blocks are produced which are added to a chain of blocks, thus giving rise to the term "blockchain". The mathematical puzzles solved are made to be sufficiently complicated while making the solution provided easy to prove. As such, each new block created can be validated quickly and the limiting factor of the network will be the rate at which mining is conducted.

2.3.2 How does Proof-of-Work and the blockchain allow Bitcoin's network to function?

There are transactions being constantly conducted on the Bitcoin network and all these transactions are gathered onto a decentralized ledger which records all current ongoing transactions. These transactions are then recorded onto blocks which are then validated across the agglomeration of miners across the world and then added to the blockchain. Apart from the current 12.5 Bitcoins awarded per block mined, miners also are paid the transaction fees paid by the transaction makers of the current block. The Bitcoin network will be undergoing a halving event on May 11, 2020, where block rewards will be slashed in half to 6.25 BTC and is expected to cause an upward pressure on price due to scarcity.

2.4 Bitcoin's promise of security

The PoW consensus algorithm allows the network to stay secure, immutable, and fair. To begin, the transaction fees charged per transaction provides a deterrent to malicious actors looking to spam the network with meaningless transactions. It would thus be extremely costly to clog up the network. Furthermore, transactions in the network cannot be forged, thus eliminating the possibility of fraud. The Bitcoin network is heavily decentralized, which means that there are thousands of Bitcoin nodes distributed globally which checks for every detail of incoming transaction data and will reject all fraudulent transactions. This is the biggest defense possible against common Distributed Denial-of-Service (DDoS) attacks carried out by hackers.

One of the only points of weakness held by Bitcoin is that it is still susceptible to 51% attacks. A 51% attack refers to attackers gaining control of 51% of the mining power in the network, thus granting them the majority computational power in the network. This allows them to reverse transactions and control the transactions that are validated and added onto the blockchain. Although this is theoretically possible, it is nearly impossible to carry out as it will take unimaginable amounts of money to set up sufficiently strong mining facilities to carry out the attack.

Furthermore, even if attackers somehow manage to coordinate a 51% attack against the network, gaining control of the network will no longer be profitable as the cryptocurrency will likely experience a massive price crash and lose its status as a secure cryptocurrency. The community will move away from using Bitcoin and the attackers are left with Bitcoins and a network that are nearly worthless and fully abandoned. It thus does not make any financial sense nor is it feasible for attacks to be carried out against the Bitcoin network, making it one of the most secure digital currencies today.

Bitcoin provides anonymity to transaction makers as well. This is because although every wallet address from every transaction carried out is recorded on the blockchain, addresses are not linked to individual identities as no form of identity has to be provided for the creation of a wallet. Provided that you keep your wallet address private, all transactions conducted by your will stay anonymous.

2.5 Fairness in Bitcoin distribution

It would be unacceptable for Bitcoin to be governed by the rich or governed by powerful entities as that would not be in line with its founding principles. For that reason, the network is made to distribute its currency in a fair manner. No one can obtain more Bitcoins simply because he owns more. Bitcoin is instead distributed proportionately to how much you are able to contribute to the network. Mining allows Bitcoins to be distributed to those who are willing to use their computational power for the betterment of the network. Despite this, critics argue that the rich will still indirectly benefit more as they can simply purchase more computing power and thus earn more.

2.6 Detractor's arguments against Bitcoin

A number of incidents involving Bitcoin has given it a bad reputation for being used largely to facilitate criminal activity. The capture of the founder of the Silk Road website, Ross Ulbricht, led to 144,000 Bitcoins being seized after a previous seizure of 26,000 Bitcoins from the users on the site. Previously, Bitcoin was being used to carry out anonymous transactions between users on the site where illegal items such as drugs, weapons, and child pornography were traded. The WannaCry ransomware attack that spread across the internet in

2017 caused more than 230,000 computers to be infected. Users had to pay a ransom of $300 worth of Bitcoin or risk the deletion of all encrypted files. These are just some of many incidents that made many disillusioned with the idea of Bitcoin and accuse it of being primarily used to support criminal organizations.

  Bitcoin enthusiasts all hope for the day where it is eventually recognized as legal tender and serves as a viable alternative to traditional currencies, much like gold. However, many argue that Bitcoin is still not ready to process transactions cheaply and quickly enough for it to effectively be referred to as a currency. As of May 9, 2020, a single transaction takes a little more than 10 minutes to be confirmed and costs an average of more than $2 per transaction. In comparison, the payment processing company Visa charges 1.51% plus $0.10 per transaction and can process over 150 million transactions per day. Bitcoin definitely has much more to improve on to match up to top payment processors. However, it has to be mentioned that Bitcoin is barely 10 years old and is consistently seeing upgrades made by the Bitcoin community of developers. Furthermore, Bitcoin has an edge in terms of privacy and security.

2.7 Bitcoin as a store of value

Bitcoin has been widely compared to gold due to its scarcity and high prices. It has a limited supply and typically performs with an inverse relationship to the economy. The deflationary characteristic of Bitcoin has allowed it to possess certain levels of insulation against the effects of a slowing economy. It shares a couple of properties with gold, the first being that it is highly interchangeable with its value recognized almost anywhere in the world. Merchants are willing to take Bitcoin as payments as they know that they can sell it for its equivalent value in local currency. Furthermore, tumultuous times like times of inflation or chaos will encourage the holding of Bitcoin instead of local currencies as seen in Venezuela and Iran. It is thus recognized as a viable store of value and is commonly referred to as digital gold.

The investment firm the specializes in digital currency trading, Grayscale Investments, was behind the 2019 campaign that sought after a shift of capital from gold to cryptocurrencies. Their executives commented that gold is now obsolete and is a relic of the physical world. In today's digital age, a digital form of gold should be adopted instead.

Despite the many properties shared with gold, Bitcoin has one flaw that detractors are quick to point out during discourse about its feasibility as a store of value. Bitcoin still experiences massive price swings up to almost half its value in a single day even in the year 2020 which makes its not a feasible store of value asset. It is likely however, that with more liquidity and adoption in future, Bitcoin will reach a price level close to its intrinsic value and lose the typical volatility associated with cryptocurrency markets. However, before that is achieved, it may be difficult for Bitcoin to prove itself as an adversary to gold.

2.8 Adoption across the world

Today, Bitcoin is used as a medium of exchange on cryptocurrency exchanges where Bitcoin can be traded for other digital currencies. Currently, the majority of Bitcoin's trading volume comes from cryptocurrency exchanges while adoption in conventional payment is on the rise daily. Bitcoin has been adopted by numerous online merchants, especially on retailers selling big ticket items who are able to absorb transaction costs. It is likely that future upgrades to the network will allow Bitcoin to see increased adoption in mainstream society which will further raise its value proposition.

One of the biggest uses of Bitcoin and other digital currencies is in the remittance industry. Traditionally, remittances from foreign workers back home are mostly conducted through financial institutions such as the Western Union. Each transaction takes days to process and often comes with ludicrous fees that diminishes a large portion of remittance values. Bitcoin today offers a much more attractive alternative, and has seen workers from countries such as Mexico, China, India, and the Philippines.

3. Blockchain

The concept of a blockchain is one of the most misunderstood concepts of today. Simply put, it is a list of records or data referred to as blocks and are linked together through cryptography. Each block of information has a cryptographic hash of the previous block in the blockchain, a timestamp that records the time of creation of the block, and a set of data recorded on the block.

3.1 Cryptography techniques

Cryptography in blockchain refers to the encryption of sensitive information through the creation of highly complicated mathematical puzzles which results in data becoming computationally secure and immutable. A cryptographic hash refers to a mathematical algorithm that converts messages, information, or data stored on the blockchain into a hash output.

The input "the red fox jumps over the blue dog" converts into an output of "DFCD 3453 BBEA 788A 751A 696C 24D9

7009 CA99 2D17". Interestingly, each code does not represent a single word and a minute change of the initial message drastically changes the final output. To illustrate, "the red fox jumps over the blue dog" gives an output of "0086 46BB FB7D CBE2 823C ACC7 6CD1 90B1 EE6E 3ABC" when passed through the mathematical algorithm. This is referred to as an avalanche effect whereby a small change can lead to a completely different output.

3.2 Cryptographic hash properties

An ideal cryptographic hash function will be able to provide its blockchain with the highest levels of security if it possesses the following few properties. The function has to be deterministic, where the same message passed through the function will yield the same result. As each block contains a cryptographic hash of the previous block, the integrity data in the blockchain can be verified and maintained with each addition of a block. The hash value should be computed quickly and should not be easily decrypted. Easy decryption leads to sensitive data on the blockchain to be exposed to malicious actors and is hence detrimental to the security of the users on the network. Lastly, no two messages should yield the same hash value as it would simply lead to confusion and false messages being recorded.

All of the above, coupled with the incorporation of the avalanche effect, provides the blockchains with one of the highest levels of information security.

3.3 Immutability

The blockchain is specifically designed to resist data modification which makes it a great tool in recording transactions for digital currencies. Unlike traditional currencies, digital currencies are not subject to risks of counterfeiting. They are also resistant to fraud as there will be fraudulent transactions will quickly be identified and rejected by validators on the network. The blockchain can be described as an open, distributed ledger that facilitates the recording of transactions between two parties efficiently in a verifiable and permanent way.

As data is being recorded on the blockchain, there is no way for data to be altered without also altering the data of all future blocks. That is a process that requires control of the network majority which is unlikely to happen. As the consensus is achieved by nodes in a peer-to-peer network, it is considered a network of decentralized and secure by design as attackers have to either gain 51% control of the network or conduct coordinated large-scale attacks on the various nodes across the world for the network to fail.

3.4 Solving the double-spending dilemma

Before the blockchain and its cryptographic hash functions were joined together to create cryptocurrencies, digital currencies were thought to be impossible to regulate and maintain due to the possibility of double-spending. Double-spending refers to an imperfection in digital currencies where the same digital token can somehow be spent more than once through forgery or duplication of tokens. The effects of double-spending can be compared to the effects of counterfeiting traditional currencies, where inflation occurs due to an excessive amount of new currency being created. Existing currency will be devalued as supply drastically increases.

The cryptographic hash functions as discussed above allow for fraudulent transactions to be flagged and rejected quickly which prevents double-spending from occurring in cryptocurrencies. Only through the solving of the double-spending dilemma, the idea of digital cash first became feasible.

4. Types of Cryptocurrencies available

Although cryptocurrencies and Bitcoin were once synonymous, the general public is becoming more informed about the industry and are now aware that there are many more cryptocurrencies available in the market other than Bitcoin. These are referred to as 'altcoins' as they are created after Bitcoin and are largely inspired by the proliferation of Bitcoin. The entire altcoin market today accounts for 32.9% of the entire cryptocurrency market capitalization as of May 9, 2020, and serves a wide assortment of purposes. With more than 5,000 projects on the market today, the market is highly saturated and competitive.

4.1 Security tokens

Security tokens are cryptocurrencies that serve similar functions to shares of a company. They are sold to the public through Initial Coin Offerings (ICOs) and represent the legal ownership of digital assets. The value of these assets are tied directly to the valuation of the issuing company and are classified as securities. As they fall under this classification, these companies will be subjected to regulation by the Securities and Exchange Commission (SEC). As such, an argument could be made for security tokens as one of the safest investment options in the industry as companies are susceptible to prosecution by the SEC should there be any attempt at scams or fraud.

The amount of red tape in the security tokens industry resulted in only certified platforms being able to facilitate security tokens trading. The current top platforms that specialize in trading security tokens are Polymath and Swarm, with projects like Blockchain Capital and 22X Fund being among the most notable projects in this category. The popularity of these projects can be seen from how the ICO of Blockchain Capital reached its cap of ten million dollars in just six hours. This is a relatively unexplored section of cryptocurrency that has large room for growth in the future.

4.2 Mining-based coins

Mining-based coins are among the most popular types of cryptocurrencies available on the market. These digital currencies function on the PoW protocol which ensures security for their networks. Most of these currencies are used to facilitate transactions and are touted as Bitcoin alternatives. Differentiation can be found in different projects from providing full anonymity to being able to process faster transactions. These projects include Monero, Litecoin, DASH, Ethereum, and ZCash.

One of the major criticisms with the PoW protocols is that massive amounts of energy have to be used to maintain networks which is considered highly wasteful. Annualized energy usage of Bitcoin is comparable to Chile's power consumption at 77.8 TWh. Bitcoin mining will also contribute to 37 Mt CO_2 in carbon footprint this year, which is equivalent to what the country of New Zealand produces. The wastage and environment degradation caused by mining has been acknowledged and there is rising interest in shifting to more power-efficient networks. Ethereum is one notable example of a project that is aiming to shift away towards a Proof-of-Stake working mechanism somewhere between 2020 and 2021.

4.3 Utility Tokens

Utility tokens are specialized currencies that allow holders to pay for the services of the host company. Filecoin and Civic are examples of such utility tokens where companies or individuals have to pay for the respective coins for data storage services and identity management processes. Utility tokens are generally considered a poor investment choice as you are essentially buying tokens from a company and then using it to pay for its services, thus keeping supply and demand relatively equal.

Despite typically not being viable investment options, utility tokens can actually increase in value if the company wants to distribute profits to token holders. This can be done through burning tokens which decreases supply of the token and raises the prices of existing tokens. However, this is extremely rare with Binance Coin being an exception. It is currently used to pay for discounted transactional fees on the Binance cryptocurrency exchange and the exchange occasionally burns a sizable supply of the coin to drive up pressure on the price of the coin.

5. Blockchain applications

Blockchain technology has many potential applications aside from being a decentralized transaction ledger. These applications can extend to across numerous sectors which will allow us to imaginably see blockchain being adopted by common businesses in the near future. Cryptocurrencies available on the market today are already able to service some the functions listed below with convincing adoption by major corporations.

5.1 Financial services

Large banks are beginning to appreciate the sophistication of blockchain technology and have acknowledged that it could prove effective in the banking industry. Through the use of distributed ledgers, banks see the potential in improving the efficiency of accounting and logistical processes. UBS, the 11th biggest bank in Europe, has funded labs to research blockchain technology to find possible applications in finance which can improve lead to greater cost-effectiveness and productive efficiencies.

Additionally, integration of blockchain is possible in the areas of asset management, insurance claims processing, and cross-border payments among many others. Other major players in finance like American Express Co., China Construction Bank, J.P. Morgan, and BNP Paribas SA have invested in blockchain in some way or another, showing that blockchain is here to stay in finance and is at best in its infancy today. The security and reliability of blockchain technology is simply a superior form of data storage that is too good to pass up in industries such as finance.

5.2 Smart contracts

Smart contracts are one of the most famous blockchain application terms used especially by Ethereum supporters. Ethereum is the second largest cryptocurrency in terms of market capitalization at about $23.5 billion and supports the execution of smart contracts executed on its blockchain. Blockchain-supported smart contracts are contracts that can be enforced automatically. A smart contract works via automated escrows, where money is sent to escrow, and will only be released to the service or goods provider after the contract is fulfilled. For instance, when purchasing an apartment through a smart contract, the escrow will only release the money to the seller after the deed is signed over to you. However, if the deed is not signed by the deadline written on the smart contract, the money is instead returned to you.

This can be done because projects like Ethereum provides developers with the ability to program their own smart contracts which can follow computational instruction. These instructions then form the basis of the agreement or contract that it is designed to enforce.

5.3 Supply chain applications

Bolstering supply chain operations has been the aim of multiple projects with numerous efforts and organizations investing in using blockchain for logistics and supply chain management. Some of the most notable projects in this area is Vechain and WaltonChain where they both hope to develop effective solutions to track logistics and incorporate technology into the manufacturing process. Walmart and IBM are among the top corporations that reportedly are investing in blockchain systems for their supply chains as well.

The immutability and integrity of a blockchain network makes it a great addition to the supply chain. This is because consensus has to be reached on data that are being added onto the blockchain. Logistical problems can now be traced to various points on the supply chain as everyone on the blockchain will have the same data on the decentralized ledger. That means that when a manufacturer has shipped out a product to be assembled in another country, all ledgers will state clearly that the product has been shipped and any problems that arises later in the supply line can be traced to specific contractors who have not had their assigned jobs recorded as completed on the ledgers.

Walmart also uses blockchain to keep records of where every piece of meat imported comes from. This allows for food safety standards to be raised considerably as each slab of meat has its processing facilities, storage facilities, and place of origin. As such, the freshness of meat can be gauged and more accurate sell-by dates can be provided to customers. This can also allow customers to identify whether the meat they are purchasing are obtained from ethically sourced farms or are cruelly extracted from poorly-run farms. This can have potential marketing and branding applications in the future that will improve the profits of existing businesses.

6. Conclusion

With the world becoming heavily digitized, digital currencies are here to stay. Cryptocurrencies created an entirely new asset class that is up and coming with increasing interest from institutional investors. Cryptocurrency investment funds are provided by hedge funds such as Fidelity Investments and given the entire market capitalization of $265 billion today, there is clearly much room for growth. It is hoped that this book can help you gain a deeper understanding about the technology behind cryptocurrency and its viability as an investable asset class. Blockchain technology will no doubt be one of the biggest breakthroughs of the 21st centuries as big data continues to expand into one of the most prominent fields today.

Understanding what cryptocurrencies and blockchains are already gives you an edge in cryptocurrency investing, as you can now conduct your own research into the various projects in the industry. Although cryptocurrencies has been referred to as the "Wild West" of the 21st century, a reference to the lawlessness of the American Old West during the mining booms, the industry has now matured from the early days of exit scams and overly unrealistic ambitions. With the help of your newfound knowledge, I believe that thorough research and analysis can also help you see the value of cryptocurrencies in the digital age and allow you to invest successfully in the industry.

Printed in Great Britain
by Amazon